CHILD

by

Deryck Grice

aquila/the phaethon press

Deryck Grice is a student teacher at The West
Midlands College of Education.   He has lived
in the West Midlands most of his life, and now
lives in Wolverhampton.

He started writing poetry some four years ago
whilst living in Liverpool.   This is his first book,
though he has been published elsewhere, and on
Radio Leicester.

This booklet is published in two editions, an
ordinary one, and a special signed edition of
26 signed and lettered copies.

SBN 903226 29 4
SBN 903226 38 3 (signed)

Published by:-

The Aquila Publishing Company Limited,
18 Atherstone Close, Shirley, Solihull, Warwicks, B90 1AU

SONG OF WAR

War Correspondent

> green landscape
> stained with red
> and sleeping bodies
> not sleeping but dead,
> the seeds in the ground
> are composed of lead.
> flashes of light
> in the night are wild
> executing our children
> without a trial,
> how could anything
> be so vile?

Child

> I am a child
> born to die.

War Correspondent

> You will learn to fall
> before you can cry.

Child

> Why?

War Correspondent

> There is no answer
> only fact.

Child

> Where is the answer?

THE CONCLUSION

Child

Where is the conclusion of death?

War Correspondent

Death is final, yet there is no conclusion.

Child

Where is the conclusion of life?

War Correspondent

In death where there is no conclusion.
There is no conclusion.
Life and death alternate between night and day,
turning like a wheel into infinity.

Child

Where is the conclusion of infinity?

War Correspondent

There is no conclusion of infinity.
It lies in red state.

Child

Where is infinity?

Infinitesimal Being

In the cold east where the asymtotes merge
and weld into cold mathematical love.
Where the people are hearded like red ants
into dreams of freedom.
Don't talk to me about infinity!

Child

There's no conclusion.

THE MESS

Child

> I shall grow old.
> You will see me in khaki grovelling
> through the bushes on my stomach,
> my seeds rubbing foreign soil.

War Correspondent

> I see blood from your mouth,
> from your mouth from your mouth
> from the north from the south
> the huge armies travel
> like dense pre-historic animals,
> then merge into passionate love,
> for death.

Child

> Stop!

War Correspondent

> The dew will come with the day
> to find a carpet of blood, spread with bodies,
> as if the morning after a party the night before.
> The dew will leave the day to mop up the mess.

Child

> I weep, for the world is a mess.

War Correspondent

> I would weep with you,
> but the tears would blurr my vision.

THE BIRTH

Child
<u></u>

    My moon flickers
    like a bulb on a television advert.

War Correspondent

    You will grow feeble and tired.
    Your mind will cease to function.

Child

    I feel like Cupid
    trying desperately to tie
    the broken string in his bow
    before his victim passes by forever.

War Correspondent

    There is no love in life.
    If you love you die.

Child

    I feel like an angel
    whose harp is all rusty and broken.
    I shall weld the strings back together
    and play music.

War Correspondent

    The strings of your life are severed.
    You decay like a cabbage in a city.
    You are rooted and invisible.

Child

    I die unknown and forgotten.
    I am born into another world.
    And where is this place
    where I,
    where I am?
    Where the window mirrors
    reflect adolescent beauty
    in a fashion,
    where the pungent smell of perfume
    drifts.
    And where is this place
    where everything is so perfect
    yet so imperfect
    Is it just to my young eyes
    that it seems so futile?

Can age be so cruel
as to bring me here?
I turn away,
but it beckons
and the current draws me
and my secondary person takes me
like a mother her child to school.
The struggle is fierce,
bloody and fierce.
Various parts of my mind
are torn from the parent mind
until it is left
exhausted and battered.
Incapable of thought.

War Correspondent

Your teachers will come
to clarify the mess
which is in your imagination.
They will teach you to become imperfect and perfect,
teach you to accept reality,
condition you into a realistic life
where you will hate,
where you will love to hate,
where hate is love.
Your laughter will be one of despair
(although you will not know it)
Go then child into the cruel city
and learn to hate.

* * * * * * *

LAND

Child

Where on this crust of concrete,
may I find a blade of natural grass,
where I may sit and graze,
without the shadow of the blocks of flats
and the multi-storey car parks
and the smouldering chimneys
and the office blocks
and where the trees will shade me
from the midday sun?
Where on this crust of concrete
may I avoid the early morning scramble,
when at dawn the workers go about their business
like a discontented child avid for still more sleep,
when at dusk they return with tails between their legs,
and tales of life's dull dregs between their teeth?

Teacher

When the night appears from nowhere,
as silent as a cat,
stars reveal themselves in rows
of vertical and horizontal uniformity. .
Grey and white reflections on walls dulled
by night's dark mysteries reveal,
life's dull uniformity.
In the town the players gather
from the buses that bring them in,
their night clothes gleaming beneath the lamplight,
in hats and shawls and long hair falling
as robes have done in darkened rooms,
where lovers lie entwined,
and the virgins lie beside their secrets.
The rattle of milk crates
on fresh white bottles
and the incessant barking dogs
awake estates from pleasant slumber;
Then into cars and onto trains and buses.
The town begins to fill,
with children unaware of breath.
The bars begin to move, the rollers begin to roll
and the chimneys light up.
The neat estates go dully about their business,
as the dogs trot the streets, and fowl the pavements.
Tradesmen call on frustrated housewives
uniformed in aprons or house-coats.
The shops are filled with novel bread
and ladies with legs not quite as fine
as once they may have been,
and life revolves, like a leather ball.

Child

On the soil the ploughs now move,
much easier than once they may have done,
and gouge out patterns on the ground
as straight as city pavements.
The worm tunnels move 'neath soil and city,
in trains of scale and man.
Where then does soil and concrete merge?

SEA

Teacher

Waves on a sea like white nippled
green breasts sucked by
vacant pockets of air reach up and up
to the illusive gulls which lie
tantalisingly just out of reach,
and sing of freedom to the water,
trapped in it's bed by gravity
and watch the waves like a lion
moving restlessly in his cage
and fly away to other parts
of the sea's vast body.

Child

The fish are learning to fly,
the planktum digging tunnels.
They plan to leave the belly bare,
the shelves will be empty in there.
Yet, when tears are shed in sorrow
for your imminent loneliness
you wage war against mankind.
Sympathy is but a catalyst for your anger,
brave and stubborn sea.

Teacher

Brave and stubborn sea,
lie silent while men cast their painless hooks,
deceptively painless hooks down your throat
and remove various parts of your stomach.
Lie silent while masked men in white coats
creep down to your beaches by the darkness
of a moonless night and urinate into your mouth
and spew into your face and spit into your eyes
and walk away counting their profits.
Lie silent while your lovers
ride on your back on saddles of wood and metal
and hurry from bank to bank
on schedules of humanity.

Child

When our fore-father's dared sail beneath your angry capes,
isolating themselves on your arid salt perimeter,
they searched for something more than this,
to use you as a weapon of war,
or for a rubbish tip.
When metal fish fathomed your depths
with all the faults of a human,
communicating death in such an ugly form,
compared to the romantic fear of your deathly storms,
did they not abuse your presence?
Do you remember those rich treasures
which were once your cargoes?
Now all you have are argosies of crude oil
which will not sink, but cover your green face,
and your blushing beaches with a colour problem.
Your dead sea captains lie beside their wrecks,
trembling, as cannisters of nerve gas fall softly
and settle by their sides,
wanting a fuck.
Brave and stubborn sea,
what answer have you to man's unquenchable thirst
for this distorted paradise?

Teacher

Waves on a sea rise like bruises
on a tortured carcass as
pipes from a tortured land
unload an excuse into a dumb body as,
unfeeling, clumsy giants collide
and spill a horrid mess as,
generals avoid concerning eyes
before unloading garbage into the green refuge tip as,
the sun revolves around unnoticed
casting shadows of sadness as
the sun casts shadows of sadness.

AND AIR

Teacher

> Black are the riddled lungs.
> Clogged is the air intake pipe.
> Immune is the filter.
> Alive is the car.
> Alive alive car.
>
> You have to be cruel to be kind
> And the truth is cruel.
> To try to take the time is cruel.
> To warn, warm or comfort is. . . . .

Child

> Is there a zoo?

Teacher

> You, you have to examine the problem
> From the core.
> We need air, air is. . . .

Child

> Is there a loo?

Teacher

> Essential to our existance.
> Analyse a sample of air,
> Find it's main pollution content,
> And. . .

Child

> And if we do.
> May I go to the loo?

Teacher

> Please do.

CHILD'S DEATH LAMENT

I looked forward to time,
time looked back at me,
i could not see where i was going.

I wandered blindly on,
could not see where time had gone,
fell into a pit of unknowing.

There i slept,
as angels wept,
until their tears revived me.

When i awoke
a girl's voice spoke,
saying where could time be.

I could not speak,
my voice was weak,
but i knew she knew the answer.

She moved away,
i begged her stay,
she said no i am a dancer.

She moved into time,
it could not be mine,
the door was closed behind her,

I moved away
as rain fell on a rainy day,
i had to search for shelter.

A damsel fair,
with rain drenched hair,
offered me her shelter.

I knew that time,
had left me far behind,
so i stayed and loved her.

Now i guess i'll never know,
where time did go,
i'll never find the answer.

i'll never find the answer,
i'll . . . .